# Do Mutton Birds Have Maps?
## and Other Poems

Jack  Harrison  Leela  Isobel  Finley  Piper and Josie

**for**

From Nanny

*& for*

The little boy who showed me the Spiderman Bird
and all other cool kids who like all creatures and poems

*From Ganga*

# Do Mutton Birds Have Maps?
## and Other Poems

**POEMS BY GANGA POWELL**
**ILLUSTRATIONS BY EILEEN CURD**

### Do Mutton Birds have Maps?

How do they make it to here
After they leave Siberia?
How do they know
where to go
When they fly
across the sky?
Do they have a star
Guiding them from far
To southern lands below
Away from sleet and snow?

Do mutton birds have diaries
Telling them when to leave
The Arctic winter freeze?
Do they see the land beneath,
Recognize the hills and plains?
Or know which mighty ocean
Is below in constant motion?
Feel the changing warming breeze
While crossing equatorial seas?

Do mutton birds have address books
To find their former nesting nooks?
How do they work out so many things
While flying along on such strong wings?

I think they have inbuilt satnav,
The very best that birds can have.

### The Kookaburra that could not Laugh

One kookaburra on an old gum tree
Happy as happy as he could be.
Then two kookaburras on the same tree
Perched together as cheeky as could be,
Laughing at something  only they could see.
Now three kookaburras all in a row,
The first one laughs and the second one too.
But the third one? Why won't he join the two?
'Laugh Kookaburra, laugh' we call,
But he sees nothing funny at all!
'Laugh Kookaburra! laugh!' we say,
'Tomorrow will be a better day!'

## Myrtle the Glamping Turtle

Myrtle the turtle
Has her house on her back
With two windows and a door
And a kayak on a rack.

She has a stove in her kitchen,
A TV in the lounge,
A fridge full of fizz
And a frilly eiderdown.

When she travels she parks
Along sandy beaches,
In camping grounds
Where fish can be found.

If the sun is shining
And the fish are biting,
She cooks some damper,
Packs her hamper,
And settles on her tartan rug
With hot coffee in her mug.

Everyone has heard
Of Myrtle the glamper
And kids love to look
Inside her camper.

## Fairy Wrens

I saw a fairy wren and then,
I saw some more
Feeding on the forest floor.
From side to side his tail he wags
While hopping along on twiggy legs.
He is as blue as a cloudless sky
With a black mask around his eye.
The others are dressed in softest velvet,
Shell pink and brown, like milky chocolate.
They all hid in the tall grass
As I tried to wriggle past.

## The Black Swans Waltz

When I went to bed last night
I saw a very special sight
As music wafted through the breeze
And softly whispered among the trees.
With red lipstick and a black dress
Mrs. Swan was out to impress.
The beat got going, one two three, swirl!
And Mr. Swan slid over to give her a twirl.
One two three swing,
This was their song,
One two three dance!
Off they pranced!
The moon and stars were shining so bright
They could not help but dance that night,
Swaying on the shimmering lake
Leaving ripples in their wake.
Soon I saw more,
First three, then four,
Five, six, seven and eight!
Oh it was so very late!
But it was a special treat to see
The swans dance so splendidly.

## Emus can't Fly

Do you know why
An emu is a bird
But cannot fly?
You see, in ages long gone by
Its legs grew longer and stronger
And its wings became smaller and weaker.

When next you see an emu
Look carefully and you
Will see two pouches, little things
On either side, the leftovers
Of what once were wings.

## The Echidna

An echidna looks like a chocolate treat
Dipped in honey and ready to eat.
But it's really not a chocolate feast,
Rather let's call it an unusual beast.

DO NOT touch or worry him please,
He will surprise you with what ease
He can roll into a ball all covered in spikes
That can attack your hands and your knees.
Then your Mum will hear you squeal
And think you have been stung by bees!

### Penguins in Suits

Black, white and stooping down
Penguins in suits belong in town
With the busy peak hour throng
Intent on work, not play, not song,
It's a hard life they seem to say
We need to get through this day.

People in the centre of town,
Crossing streets with heads down
Looking like penguins on parade.
I wonder if all their suits were made
In the same shop that outfits
Smart little penguin chicks?

For colouring in ...

## Two Tawny Frogmouths

I think I can, I think I see
A tawny Frogmouth on that tree.
Or is it a grey-brown bit of bark
Peeling off the tree, you ask.
But that wide lip and cross old scowl?

It has to be a Frogmouth, not an owl.
'Woooo!' you cried
And four brown eyes opened wide,
Not one but two Frogmouths!
'Woooo! Whooo!'

# Magpies at Dawn

Have you ever woken up at dawn
And heard the magpie's morning song?
Welcoming the golden sun
Without which the earth won't run,
Rising from his clouds of pillows
From the sea beneath that billows
Like a crumpled eiderdown.
Who can copy the magpie's song?

On a drum? A banjo?
A fiddle? A lute?
Perhaps on a piccolo or a flute
Piping a melodious note.
Or a little boy's treble
Effortless as a bubble,
Raised in praise
Of the magpie's song.

# Dolphins Frolicking in the Bay

Dolphins frolicking in the bay
On a warm and sunny day.
Arcing across the turquoise water
Bringing smiles of joy and laughter
To the people on the beach,
Gathering to see what each
Could etch into their memory
Of dolphins playing in the sea.
Sparkling water, arching backs,
Snow white spray marking their tracks,
Speckled silver by the sun.
Now the dolphins are on the run,
Sleek and slick they dive and surface,
Then off they race to another place!

# Rainbows and Butterflies

Do you know
Where butterflies go
When winter sets in
And there is snow?
I think they hide in rainbows
Arching through the sky
Waiting for a summery day
When they can flutter by.
Violet, yellow, blue and green
All their colours can be seen
In rainbows across the sky
Until winter has gone by.
Then the warm and welcoming sun
Urges them to have some fun,
To dance, flutter wings and sing
And make the most
Of the coming of spring.

## Cheeky Cockies

Cheeky cockies in the trees
Swaying in the southern breeze.
Raucous caucus of noisy birds
Fighting over roosting spaces
Among the Norfolk island pines;
As the fading evening washes
Trees, river, streets and town
In the mellow yellow
Of the setting sun.
Shhhh....
Quiet at last as cockatoos
Settle to their nightly snooze.
Do not wake them up I pray
Until we get to another day!

## The Spiderman Bird

"Look! Look! A Spiderman Bird!"
Said a little boy whom I overheard.
I looked and saw what he had seen:
Hidden among the leaves of green
A bird in a suit of red and blue.

I thought it looked like Spiderman too.
Then with a swish and a whoosh it flew,
One minute it was there, then it was gone
Possibly to rescue a bird forlorn,
Off on a Spiderman Bird mission
That had come to its attention.

## The Wallaby under the Willow

The wallaby under the willow
Is a friendly little fellow,
Following us with marble eyes
I think we took him by surprise!

His ears are pointy,
His paws disjointy,
His whiskers move slightly,
Ever so lightly.
Then a commotion

Sets him in motion
Hop, skip and jump!
Away over the hump!

## Penguin Parade

Penguins in line
Waddling up the sand
Make me want
To give them a hand.
Stumbling over wrinkles,
Falling into furrows,
An obstacle course as they
Hurry to their burrows.

Hold my hand
You absurd bird,
Before you roll back
To the start of the track.
If you do, well then
You'll have to start
All over again!

## Pelicans

Pelicans like a line of schoolboys,
In white shirts and black blazers,
hair slicked back, all very smart
You can hardly tell them apart;
Except for one a bit more unkempt
Who had given up after one attempt.
He needs some gel you can tell,
For those feathers that are hard to quell.

Eileen Curd.

# Cheep! Cheep! Cheep!

A fulltime job for magpie dad and magpie mum
Is filling their big, growing chick's tum.
'Cheep! Cheep! Cheep!' says the magpie chick
Desperately trying to eat a stick.
There's his Daddy feeding him a worm
While his Mum is digging up a storm.
Here she comes, she's got an insect,
Really, what more does he expect?

But 'Cheep! Cheep! Cheep!' he cries
And to eat the stick again he tries.
I wonder what your Mum would say
If you went 'Cheep! Cheep! Cheep!' all day?
And your Dad?
Wouldn't he be mad?!
There he goes, the magpie chick,
'Cheep! Cheep! Cheep!

www.ingramcontent.com/pod-product-compliance
Lightning Source LLC
Chambersburg PA
CBHW041154290426
44108CB00002B/67